INTRO

MW01126181

INDIA

Culture and Traditions of India

India Guide Book

Shalu Sharma

ISBN-13: 978-1983540493
ISBN-10: 1983540498

Other books by the author: https://www.amazon.com/author/shalusharma

Hinduism For Kids: Beliefs And Practices
India For Kids: Amazing Facts About India
Hinduism for Beginners
An Introduction to the Way of the Buddha
Essential India Travel Guide
All about India: Introduction to India for Kids
India For Children
Third Eye Awakening
Hinduism Made Easy
Essential Hindi Words And Phrases For Travelers
India Travel Health Guide

Table of Contents

Introduction to India

India is a nation located in South Asia often referred to as a subcontinent. By landmass, it is the seventh-largest nation as well. The subcontinent is surrounded by the Arabian Sea, the Bay of Bengal and the Indian Ocean to the south. In the north, it has a land border that connects with China, Pakistan, Bhutan, Bangladesh, Myanmar, and Nepal. India's unique geographical position puts it in a perfect place to enter many different trade markets. It also makes it one of the easiest countries to identify on a map.

India is a country that has a long history that dates back thousands of years. In fact, archaeologists have discovered evidence of human beings existing in India about 75,000 years ago. So the land that India sits on definitely has a history that is older than the country itself. As for ancient India, this was a time period that spawned four major religions that are still used today; Sikhism, Buddhism, Jainism and Hinduism. These are some of the oldest known religions in the world and have helped countless people over the centuries in finding peace of mind and serenity. They have even spread beyond India's borders and into other regions of the world.

India is a very diverse country in both landscape and people. It is made up of 26 states which have all different kinds of landscapes, similar to how the United States does. But in India, you will find mountain ranges, deserts, beaches, grasslands, jungles and national parks. This gives tourists and locals so many things to do and places to visit. And because of the many borders it shares with various other nations, including China, this makes India a popular destination for immigrants and migrants alike. One of the big reasons why India has so many diverse people in it is because of their northern borders they share with other countries. This gives foreigners an easy way to get to India since they likely cannot afford to fly anyway. Thousands of years before flight travel even existed, India still experienced immigration. But they also had people leaving the country as well, which is why many ancient Indian religions spread across the world. In fact, it is why China now has more Buddhists living in their country than India does.

There are a lot of stereotypes and misinterpretations about India. People in the west often assume India is a very poor country that is in the ranks of being a third world country. Although there are millions of poor people in the country, it actually has a fast growing economy. It is considered to be the 7th largest in the world by nominal GDP. This is mainly due to its industrialization and globalization. Of course, it still has problems when it comes to malnutrition, corruption, healthcare, and poverty. But you have to remember that it is a country with over a billion people in it, which means you are always going to have these kinds of problems with a country that populated.

If you look at China, for example, they have 1.35 billion people and are considered to have the 2nd biggest economy in the world. And yet, they still have millions of poor people working for slave wages and struggling to get by. India is pretty much in the same boat. They have many poor people, despite having a thriving economy. But if you were to go to the big cities in India then you would see a lot of international franchises and big businesses which cater to tourists. So if you are ever thinking about going to India then do not be put off by the rumors of it being a third world country. It is a thriving country with diversity and historic beauty that everyone in the world should experience at least once in their lives.

People of India

As of today, India has more than 1.32 billion people residing in the country, which makes it the second-most populous nation on Earth. They are just behind China which has 1.37 billion people. However, the Indian people are much more diverse than the Chinese people and are spread out amongst different regions into ethno linguistic groups. Since India has a vast history of immigration and British dominance, this created a lot of diversity amongst the traditional Indian people. This diversity is also influence by the variety of religions, climates, and cultures of the country. Over the years, these influences ultimately changed people in these regions in a way that made them unique from those in other regions of the country. That is what made the caste system so successful in the country. It allowed people of similar nationalities and backgrounds to stick together in their closely knitted communities. That way the only way they knew how to survive. There are some Indian people that still choose to stay in these communities even to this day. But you will find them away from the major cities of the country.

Part of the Indian diversity comes with its languages. The two most widely used languages in India are Hindi and English. Hindi is the traditional language of India that you will find used privately amongst Indian citizens when they are talking to each other. Northern India uses Hindi more than any other region of the country. As for English, this is their other official language that is used for governmental and business purposes. Since English is a widely accepted language around the world, this gives the Indian people a chance to better communicate with foreigners and conduct more business transactions with them. However, the Indian Constitution has named 14 other official regional languages besides Hindi. There is Assamese, Bengali, Malayalam, Gujarati, Marathi, Kannada, Punjabi, Kashmiri, Tamil, Oriya, Sindhi, Telugu, Urdu and Sanskrit. These are just the official regional languages though. India actually has more than 1,500 languages and dialects used in total. The majority of these languages come from tribal people who live away from civilization and have adapted their own forms of communication that people outside their community do not speak. It is their way of staying closely together and not allowing outsiders to interfere with their people or way of life.

Many people assume that Indian is a type of race, but it is not. The Indian people are made up of four races; Caucasian, Asian, Black and Australoid. If you were going to be technical about it, you would refer to Indians as Asians because India is part of the Asian continent. But the truth is that Indians are closer to the Caucasian race than anything else. This was concluded after the genes and skulls of various Indian remains were studied and found to be Caucasoid. However, it would be hard to get the general public to accept this because they only judge people by skin color. Caucasians are mostly viewed as having white skin, which Indians do not have. But scientists believe that the climate and living conditions have a lot to do with the evolving skin color. Not only that, emigration from Europe also had something to do with this. As more races started living together and reproducing, this changed the DNA of the Indian race tremendously. In northern India, you typically have traditional looking Asian people there because of this region's close proximity to the borders of other Asian countries. As you go further south, you'll have a variety of mixed Indians with Caucasian and African ancestry to them.

History of India

The history of India can be traced back to 73,000 B.C. Of course it wasn't an actual country at that time, but there were people living on the land back then. But as far as the oldest Indian civilization goes, archaeologists have found ancient scriptures which they have dated to be from 3,000 B.C. At this time, the Indus Valley Civilization was residing in Pakistan and the northwest region of India. But there wasn't much of an urban culture at this point. It wasn't until 2,600 B.C. that people started to become more technologically savvy by constructing urban centers and marketplaces. But the Indus Valley Civilization was short lived and eventually fell apart. In 1,900 B.C. the first political territory was formed by the Iron Age Vedic Civilization of the North Indian River Plain. This civilization formed sixteen kingdoms to govern this territory. Mahajanapadas is the word that describes how northern India became more of a political region of the country. Every other region of the country was still uncivilized and ungoverned at this point. Then civilization slowly spread to the south over the next thousand years.

Perhaps the most prominent figure of Indian history was Siddhartha Gautama, also known as Buddha. He lived around 650 B.C. and is viewed as an inspirational figure for teaching others about how to reduce their suffering and increase their peace of mind. Buddha's teachings were later formed into the religion now known as Buddhism. As far as ancient religions go, Buddhism is one of the oldest religions in the entire world. It is also a unique religion because it does not worship any particular god or divine entity. Instead, Buddhists are taught to be nice to others and refrain from becoming materialistic. By doing so, they will find happiness in the physical world and their spirit will get closer to enlightenment in the spiritual world after they are dead. This gives Buddhists an incentive to be faithful to the teachings of Buddha so that one day their spirit will achieve enlightenment as well.

In modern Indian history, the most notable figure of the last
100 years would be Mahatma Gandhi. He was the one who led
Indians into an independence movement against the British,

who had dominated their country for centuries. At first, there were European trading companies simply going to India for business purposes. But the vast amount of wealth that the Europeans had ended up taking over the Indian marketplaces. Eventually, British businesses began settling in India with their enormous wealth and put the small business people of India out of business. It eventually got to the point where the British's wealth helped influence the social, economic and political ways of Indian life. This was what ultimately allowed them to take over the country in the 19th century after bringing political figures and military troops to the country. At this point, the British were taking advantage of India by draining their natural resources for their own commercial gain. The British also forced the Indian people to conduct slave labor for them as well.

In 1947, the British left India after Gandhi inspired the Indian people to continue demanding independence from them. What is most memorable was that he did this while telling the

Indian people not to be violent toward the British. Instead, he convinced them to not be influenced by them and to accept whatever lashings or punishments they have to endure for their disobedience. Once the British realized they did not have influence over the Indian people anymore, this ultimately led them to retreat from the country and give independence back to the people.

Hinduism- The main religion of India

Hinduism is one of the oldest religions to come out of India. On a worldwide scale, it is the 3rd most followed religion with just over 850 million followers. This puts it behind Christianity which is the 1st most followed religion with 2.1 billion followers, and Islam which is the 2nd most followed religion with 1.3 billion followers. The majority of the world's Hindus live in India where the religion was started. In fact, 80% of the Indian people are Hindus. Since there are 1.3 billion people living in India, then roughly 1 billion of them identify as Hindu. Try to imagine a population that is 3 times the size of the U.S. population believing in Hinduism, and all in the same country. That is quite a lot of people to consider. But it explains why Hinduism is such an influential part of Indian culture and why many Hindu beliefs are practiced on the streets in every major city in the country. This is why you will see cows roaming the streets and being let free, since Hindus believe cows are sacred. This is how powerful Hinduism is in the everyday life of the Indian people.

There are some Indian states that will prosecute people for breaking certain Hindu traditions, like killing cows. But for the most part the choice to respect cows and follow other Hindu beliefs is really a personal choice more than anything else. Truly devoted Hindus wouldn't want to break these traditions because they are afraid of being reincarnated into a worse life after their current life ends. Hindus believe if they don't assault, steal or kill then they will be rewarded in the afterlife by being reborn into a better life. Then as they keep their karma strong and positive, they will eventually achieve enlightenment. This is when their soul will be at peace for all eternity. Every Hindu wants to achieve them and the belief in this is what motivates them to stick to the traditions. That is why the Indian government rarely ever has to enforce any laws that pertain to Hindu traditions because people will follow them on their own for the most part.

The largest collection of Hindu scriptures is known as the Vedas. The scriptures in this collection date back as far as 1,500 B.C., but they could possibly be even older than that. They are written in an extinct language called Vedic Sanskrit, which is believed to be the first Sanskrit language and the first one that Hindus used for their scriptures. All of the teachings of Hinduism that are still used today are derived from the Vedas. These scriptures are as important to Hindus as the Holy Bible is to Christians. The difference is the Vedas is 1,000 years older than the Bible. Another difference is Hinduism doesn't have any declared founder nor does it have just one God. The religion has their main god called "Brahman," the Supreme Being but there are also other gods which are manifestations of Brahman. These gods include Shiva, Rama, Parvati, Ganesha, Krishna and Saraswati just to name a few. All Hindus worship Brahman and believe he exists in just about everything and everyone. Whether it is an object or a God, the power of Brahman is in all of them. Those who accept

Brahman's power for what it is will also be brought closer to enlightenment. It isn't enough to just be kind to others and not hurt anyone. You have to accept Brahman's energy in everything and allow your spirit to connect with it. Without that spiritual connection, you will never be able to find enlightenment. Instead you will just keep getting reincarnated again and again until you finally do accept his power.

Caste system of India

When the Indian Constitution was written in 1949 and enacted in 1950, it stated that all the citizens of India have equal rights under the newly passed legislation. This was a big change from the caste system that the country had used for many centuries. In fact, the caste system dates back all the way to ancient times. This was when religion and wealth what separated people. The caste system was certainly not about equal rights for all. Instead, it was a Hindu-based system where people were divided into different social classes based on their popularity, occupation, wealth and income. These were often hereditary classes where generations of families stayed within the same social class without any chance of breaking out of it and moving onto a new class. In other words, if you came from a poor family with minimal education then you had virtually no chance of escaping poverty and rising to an upper class lifestyle. These groups under the caste system were called jatis, or simply just castes.

By the start of the 20th century, there were more than 1,600 castes throughout India. But the first big change to this system occurred when Indians were inspired by Gandhi to start a movement for independence from their British rulers. What they wanted was more than just to drive the British away. They wanted equality for themselves without being dominated by those with more wealth and power than they had. Once the Indian independence movement began, the caste system started to crumble throughout major Indian cities. After the Indian Constitution was put into law then the caste system became virtually nonexistent. The caste system does still exist in some rural areas of the country where people don't normally go. However, the Union Government of India is far too limited in its resources to actually send law enforcement officials out to these rural areas to enforce the law. So they just let the people of these areas go about their business and take care of themselves. This means all of the food, water, clothing and shelter has to be produced by the people of these areas because the government doesn't assist them.

The caste system can be viewed as both good and bad. Many wonder why people in the rural areas of India would choose to stay there and not go to one of the bigger cities where they would be treated as equals. Well for starters, those raised in rural areas under a caste system don't know any other way of life. All they know is the people of their community and what they are taught by them. If they were to go outside of this community then they would be lost and alone. That is why Indian tribal communities and indigenous people still exist there today. They would rather stay amongst those of their own social class because they can relate to them the most.

The Indian Constitution prohibits discrimination against those of the lower caste levels, which are basically poorer Indians with little social status. However, caste identities are still relevant in modern Indian society even though people are supposed to have equal rights. But the caste system affects people personally more than legally. Marriage is an example of this. According to a 2005 census, only 11% of Indian women chose to marry someone of a different caste than them. All of the rest married men of the same caste, which was likely influenced by the pressures of their social class to marry someone like them. As for job opportunities, lower caste people are supposed to be able to move up the economic ladder and get better jobs. But there are reports of them still being discriminated against, despite that being against the law. The Union Government rarely prosecutes people for this discrimination too.

Cricket – The most popular sport in India

Many countries have popular sporting games that help shape their culture. In America, football and basketball are the two most popular sports in the country. In India, the most popular sport is cricket. The majority of the Indian people play cricket, whether it is professionally or for fun. Cricket in India was first made popular in 1918. This was at a time in India when the country was still dominated by the British. In fact, the earliest record of the existence of cricket can be traced back to 16th century England. This was a game that used to be played by English royalty such as Prince Edward. In the year 1600, Britain's East India Company was given a Royal Charter by Queen Elizabeth to conduct trade in the East Indies. Ultimately, the company ended up doing trade with China and India. With all of the company's wealth and power, they founded the city now known as Madras. On the western Indian coast, they even acquired the Portuguese territory there which included Bombay. In 1690, English merchants went to the Hooghly River to establish a trading settlement under the permission of the Anglo-Moghul treaty. This area would eventually become modern day Calcutta.

When the British government's troops arrived in India they started a commercial trading venture with them which ended up dominating the country. This allowed Britain's culture to influence the Indian culture to the point where the Indian people started adapting customs introduced to them by the British people. One of these customs was playing the game of cricket for sport. Each Indian location the British took over for trading purposes became huge cricket centers. The native population found a unique liking to the game that they had never experienced before. It also gave poorer people something to do in their leisure time that was fun and competitive in the communities they lived in. It helped take their minds off the tough living conditions they endured on a daily basis, especially under the rule of the British.

First-class cricket is the term used to describe a professional game of cricket where there are actually domestic and international standards put in place for the game. It is when teams play each other while being observed by judges who are keeping score. The Europeans were the team of the British and the Parsees were the team of Indians, although the Parsees were actually of Persian Zoroastrian descent who immigrated to India. In the season of 1892-1893, the Europeans and Parsees had their first matches in the first-class cricket arena. The games were held in Bombay and Poona. The Parsees were declared the winning team of that particular season, but then the Europeans dominated the wins over the next four seasons. The Parsees did go on to tour other countries and play cricket in them. As for the Europeans in

India, they couldn't believe how well the Indian people were doing at this game.

In 1932, the national cricket team of India had their first test match at Lord's Cricket Ground in London, England. They were considered one of the weaker cricket teams when held to international standards. But in the 1970s, the team started to turn itself around with prominent batsmen like Gundappa Viswanath and Sunil Gavaskar. This allowed them to improve their playing performance against foreign competitors and ultimately led them to win the Cricket World Cup in 1983, and then again in 2011. As of today, India is ranked first out of all the test-playing countries in the world. Many Indian families, both poor and rich, love to play cricket out on the streets for fun no matter where they are. That is how much of an influence the game has on the lives of the Indian people.

Indian food – What Indians eat and how

The regions of India have become very diverse because of all the immigration the nation has experienced over the centuries. Everyone who has come to India has brought their own cultural experiences and knowledge with them. This has greatly influenced the type of Indian food that comes out of the country. Not only that, the diverse climates throughout the various regions of India have also influenced the way food is grown there. This, in turn, affects what the people eat and the food choices they have available in each region. That is why when you travel throughout the northern and southern regions of India, you will find vast differences in the types of fruits, vegetables, spices and herbs that are offered at restaurants.

The one thing that Indian food and recipes do have in common is that they are influenced by people's Dharmic beliefs. The word "Dharma" comes from many of the ancient Indian religions such as Sikhism, Hinduism, Janisim and Buddhism. However, those of each faith give a different meaning to Dharma and what the word represents. Overall, the word represents people's particular religious views towards things like food and lifestyle. Dharma has no actual meaning in Western society, but to Indians it is taken seriously because it is a reflection of their culture and traditions. The best example of this is with people's views towards cow. The Dharmic beliefs of Hindus are that cows are sacred and should not be used for beef. That is why Hindu restaurants have mostly vegetarian food choices like chickpeas, paneer (cheese), spinach and spicy potato curry. Religion is an influential force when it comes to what foods people serve. The rest of the influences have to do with agriculture and ethnic culture.

Throughout the 20th and early 21st century, globalization began to influence Indian food somewhat. If you were to go to New Delhi then you would see American restaurant franchises like Burger King, Domino's and McDonalds. This has added even more diversity to the food choices in India. However, the actual food choices at these American-based restaurants are not going to be the same as you would find in the actual restaurants in the United States. For example, a McDonalds in the U.S. will typically have hamburger food choices like a Big Mac. Since Indians don't like to eat cow meat, you aren't going to find foods at the Indian McDonalds with hamburger meat in them. So instead of the Big Mac with multiple beef patties, you will see the Chicken Maharaja Mac as its chicken alternative. There is also the Veg Maharaja Mac which is the vegetarian version of the Big Mac. These changes allow international food chains to cater to the food demands of the locals. If McDonalds were to force their restaurants in India to serve hamburgers with beef then they obviously wouldn't get very many customers. So adapting their menus to the local customs of India is beneficial for these food chains.

The majority of the Indian population lives off rice, wheat, lentils and vegetables. Even if they wanted to be meat eaters, it would be too costly and time consuming for them to have to raise animals for meat. Many people are poor in India so they are forced to feed themselves with cheap food that is easy to grow. Rice and lentils are definitely at the top of that list. In fact, rice is considered to be a staple food in India. It is about just as popular there as it is in China, which is also a neighboring country to India. China has a lot of poor people too that live off rice to survive because it's cheap. Many say that Chinese immigrants who moved to India helped adapt the popularity of rice into the country.

Indian women: Arranged marriages and the dowry system

Women in India used to be second class citizens who would get forced into arranged marriages. Some of these customs still exist in certain backward rural areas of India, but there are liberated women too and things are beginning to change in modern India. However, the liberation of a woman has more to do with their family than anything else. The dowry system is still predominately used in Indian families. This is an ancient system where money or property is given to the parents of the groom by the bride's father in exchange for their daughter's hand in marriage.

Usually, you will see poorer Indian families taking advantage of this system because it is an easy way for them to make money and ensure their daughter is well taken care of in the future. As for middle and upper class Indian women and their families, they tend to support equal rights for women. In fact, there are numerous examples where Indian women have actually held public office. Women have served as President, Leader of the Opposition, Speaker of the Lok Sabha (Lower House of Parliament), Chief Minister, Governor, and Union Minister. Some believe that western influences helped give women a chance to make names for themselves in India.

The biggest reason why women have equal rights is because of the Indian Constitution that was enacted after the nation declared its independence from the British. In the Indian Constitution, it states that women have equal rights and the freedom to not be subjected to discrimination. There are even more descriptive statutes of the constitution which govern women's rights. However, enforcing the laws surrounding women's rights has been a challenge in India over the last 60 years since the constitution was written. This has to do with the country's limited funding for policing and law enforcement resources which would otherwise enable them to protect women better. From time to time Indian women are still subjected to numerous violent attacks. These attacks occur more commonly in areas which have virtually no police presence at all, such as rural areas.

There are some reports of dowry killings and even acid throwing in India. The problem with the dowry system is that it can easily subject young Indian girls to abuse. For example, western societies typically make girls wait until they are 18-years-old before they can legally get married. In India, their legislation says that a young girl has to be 18-years-old as well. But because of the country's poor law enforcement, child marriages occur frequently in India. When it happens under the dowry system, it could mean the young girl gets taken into a new family without her will. As for the girl's family, they don't think about the risks so much because of what they get offered for their daughter marrying their son. This is why the dowry system is a bad system that is open to potential abuses towards women and young girls.

On a lighter note, most arranged marriages have a happy ending. Mine was also an arranged marriage. Potential brides and grooms now meet each other before making up their minds to get married or not. Many girls and boys wait till they get a job before committing to getting married. The most common arranged marriages are those that occur when a girl reaches her 18th birthday and the boy reaches his 21st birthday. This is the way legally arranged marriages occur in India. Of course, some families may arrange for their children to marry earlier than that. Marriages between 12-year-old girls and 14-year-old boys are typically common in India, despite it being against the law. But again, it is rare that any law enforcement official would actually stop them.

Bollywood – The film industry of India

You are probably familiar with "Hollywood," which is a neighborhood in Los Angeles that is known for being the headquarters of the American film industry. But what you may not realize is that other countries have their own version of Hollywood. In India, their film industry headquarters is located in the city of Mumbai. This area has been given the nickname "Bollywood," which is a pun on the Hollywood name. The "B" stands for Bombay, which is what the city of Mumbai used to be called. So they basically just took the "H" off Hollywood and replaced it with "B."

Bollywood isn't the only place in India where films are made, though. There are also Indian film production companies in West Bengal, Assam, Punjab, Haryana and Tamil Nadu. However, the reason why Bollywood gets so much attention, besides its name, is because it is the central location for Hindi film productions. Since there are millions of people living in India that actually speak the Hindi language, this makes Hindi films the dominate ones out of all the rest in the country. Sure there are English films made there too, but those who know the Hindi language prefer seeing films where the actors actually speak Hindi.

Film production in India isn't exactly a new thing. They have actually had films being made there just about as long as Americans have been making films in the United States. The only difference is now we live in a more globalized society where we have the internet to share multimedia content throughout the world. This has allowed people outside of India to discover Bollywood and many of the films they produce. But before then, most Hindi films were exclusive to India only. The first Bollywood film to get produced was in 1913. The film was called "Raja Harishchandra." There were only a limited number of screenings of this film at the time since cinema was still in the dark ages in India. But for those who did see it, they were amazed to see such moving images on a screen for the first time. The enthusiasm from audiences inspired Bollywood to keep on going with their film productions.

Over the next two decades, Bollywood was starting to produce even more films. By the 1930s, more than 200 films per year were being produced there. The first Indian film to have sound was called "Alam Ara," which came out in 1931. To the Indian people, this film was revolutionary because they had never seen a movie with sound before. Alam Ara became very popular for that reason and it is still viewed by film historians as the turning point for the Indian film industry.

That film led to a series of other film productions in Bollywood that were talkie films and musicals. Then other cities throughout India started developing their own film production companies. However, the late 1930s and 1940s were a tough time for India because they were forming the Indian independence movement along with the aftershocks of the Great Depression and World War II. Bollywood ended up using these social issues as topics and plots for their next films.

After World War II ended in 1945, the films that came out of Bollywood started to become influenced by Western films and culture. Bollywood films were even being shown at international film festivals for the first time. Hindi films were finally recognized after the Bollywood film "Neecha Nagar" was up for an award at the first Cannes Film Festival and won the Grand Prize there. This is when people around the world starting using the name "Bollywood" to refer to Hindi films coming out of India. Now the name is used just as often as Hollywood is used. Anyone with an internet connection can now experience these films and appreciate where they came from.

The cow – India's holy animal

If you live in the western world then you probably don't think too much about cows because they are just used for food there. Anytime you go into a supermarket and see beef or steak wrapped up in cellophane, you know it came from a cow. But in Indian culture, cows are viewed as sacred by the people there. This is one of the reasons why many Indians are vegetarians for the most part. If Indians are going to eat any kind of meat it will be chicken or some form of white meat. But one thing you won't see is an Indian eating the meat of a cow. This goes back to the Hindu culture of the country which 80% of its people follow. The influence of Hinduism has allowed cows to become liberated and free, so to speak. That is why you can see wild cows roaming the streets. People are not afraid to leave them alone and let them wander about on their own. This is something you would never see happen in a western society.

Hindus do not actually worship cows. This is a common misconception of people outside of India when they hear about cows roaming Indian streets. Hindus simply have a deep respect for cows. However, cows do serve other agricultural purposes to Indian people when they are kept alive. Cows are still used to produce dairy products, such as milk, and their dung is used as a source of fertilizer and fuel. Hindus view cows as maternal figures in a way because they can produce these resources for them. The Hindu goddess known as "Bhoomi" is represented in the form of a cow because they believe her spirit rests within them. In fact, many Hindus associate the gentle nature of cows with the main teaching of Hinduism which tells people not to cause injury to others. Since cows would never intentionally harm a human being, Hindus believe they are driven by a divine spirit that keeps them at peace.

Despite the fact that 80% of the Indian population is Hindus, there are some parts of the subcontinent where they do consume beef. In Tamil Nadu and Kerala, for example, there are many Hindus that will eat beef. But in the Indian state of Maharashtra, they have fully outlawed the consumption of beef. In fact, you cannot even possess cow meat there or else you will get arrested. But most people there couldn't afford their own cows anyway. That is why cows are actually used more for monetary purposes and trade than anything else. If a person is seen walking down the street with a pet cow, they are looked at as upper class and admired by those around them. Then if that person ever needed money quickly they could sell their cow and make a good sum of cash.

In Hinduism, cows are more than just an animal. They are a symbol of every other creature on earth including birds, fishes and mammals. Since cows two primary functions are feeding and giving, Hindus see that as a representation of life and the ability to sustain life. Hindus draw inspiration from these cows which help them be gentle and kind to other people and animals of nature. Cows have been respected by Hindus like this since the Vedas scriptures were first written. Respect for cows can be read in virtually all the ancient Hindu scriptures. Even though you will read in these scriptures that Hindus ate deer, fish, and numerous other animals, you will never read about them eating cow meat. This is one tradition of Hinduism that has not changed in 3000 years and it likely won't change anytime soon.

Best places to visit in India for cultural experience

India is one of the oldest countries in the world which means it contains many great historical monuments and cultural attractions. People from all over the world visit India each year to experience these attractions. However, if you're going to make the trip worthwhile and get a feel for the true Indian culture, then you need to visit the right locations. The Chand Baori, for example, is an ancient stepwell located in the village of Abhaneri, Rajasthan. The stepwell was built in the 10th century and contains 11 levels to it, with each level having a depth of 20 meters. When you go to visit this stepwell, you will be absolutely stunned by the beauty of its architectural design. While you're in the village of Abhaneri, you can also visit its temple and small palace which is located near the Chand Baori. You'll notice all of the villagers reside in mud huts. Even though they are practically living in poverty, the villagers are very nice and will be honored to show you the inside of their homes. It doesn't get more cultural than this.

The northern Indian city of Amritsar is another cultural
hotspot you should go and visit. Amritsar is where the Sikh
religion was born, so you will find a great number of Sikhs in
this area and you can see how they live. Do not worry because
the people of this city are very welcoming to tourists and
travelers. One of the biggest attractions in the city is the
Golden Temple, which is very easy to spot because it can be
seen in the skyline and it is one of the few buildings that is the
color of gold. The temple is one of the holiest places where
Sikhs go to pray and worship. Later on, if you're hungry, you
can dine at one of the many snack bars in the city and meet
the locals there. The most popular snack bar is called the
Brothers Dhaba. They sell a variety of delicious cultural
delicacies that you'll be sure to enjoy.

A trip to India wouldn't be complete without visiting its largest city. Kolkata, formerly known as Calcutta, used to be the capital of India and contains a vast amount of cultural festivals, art galleries, and colonial architecture. If you want to learn about the history of Indian culture, then you have to visit Kolkata. One attraction in particular that actually draws a lot of tourists is the South Park Street British Cemetery. Although it's not formerly a tourist attraction, if you give the gatekeeper a small donation then he'll let you inside. Once you enter the cemetery, you will feel like you're in a completely different world. It is filled with tall trees, huge graves, and tombs where hundreds of British soldiers are buried. There are also anglicized cenotaphs that are about 400 years old. Many of the fallen British were young men and women who died of disease or illness.

Lastly, a visit to the Old Birla House in New Delhi is essential in order to appreciate the revolution that India went through in the middle of the 20th century. Mahatma Gandhi was killed in 1948 at the Old Birla House. Although this was a horrible event, the house itself has been turned into a beautiful building that now serves as a museum dedicated to Gandhi's memory. The house contains his Spartan furniture, a cabinet full of Gandhi's old "worldly goods," and a series of concrete footsteps which outlines the exact path that Gandhi walked before he was killed. The house is also filled with photos and literature on the wall which document Gandhi's last days and his significance on the independence that India achieved because of his efforts.

Varanasi is one of the holiest places for the Hindus of India. It is also the oldest city known to be continuously inhabited anywhere in the world. It has been known by other names throughout its history such as Kashi and then Benaras or Banaras. The pilgrimage center is situated on the banks of the holy River Ganges. The city is of religious importance to Jains and Buddhists in addition to being the salvation ground of Hindus. If you want to understand the culture of India then you might wish to visit this city.

Languages of India

India is a very diverse country with people from many different cultures and backgrounds. According to a census that was conducted in 2001, the country of India has a total of 122 widely-used languages and approximately 1,599 minor languages. All these languages are part of many different language families. About 75% of all Indian people speak one of the Indo-Aryan languages and 20% of all Indian people speak one of the Dravidian languages. Some of the other language groups include Tai-Kadai, Sino-Tibetan, and Austroasiatic. Other minor language families are only used indigenously in certain desolate areas of India.

The two officially used languages of India are Hindi and English. The Constitution of India has not actually declared these two languages to be the official languages of the country, though. But they are both used by officials of the

Indian government when they conduct parliamentary proceedings, judiciary proceedings, and when they communicate with state governments. About 14.5% to 24.5% of the entire Indian population are native Hindi speakers. Roughly 45% of the population speak a certain dialect of Hindi.

As for English, this became more widely used at the federal level during the era of the British Raj. This was an era from 1858 to 1947 when the British ruled the entire Indian subcontinent. Once the Indian constitution was created after the country got its independence, it foresaw that Hindi would eventually be replaced with English. Some people wanted to keep Hindi as the only official language of India, but this idea was not liked in certain regions of the country where English was more popular. So now, both languages are widely used today.

The states of India have the power to declare their own official languages. Because of this, there are 22 official languages in India that are spread out amongst these states. Some of these states have English and Hindi as their official languages while others have different official languages. Most of the other official languages are ones that people outside of Asia have never heard of before. These include the languages of Kannada, Marathi, Meiteilon, Punjabi, Odia, Mizo, Bengali, Kokborok, Urdu, Tamil, and Telugu. Some of the languages are spoken only in certain regions of India and others, like Punjabi, come from south Asian countries like Pakistan. A lot of the immigration that India has had over the centuries is mainly responsible for their vast diversity in languages and culture.

The languages of India are very complicated because there have been so many spoken over the last 2000 years and beyond. The Government of India has even gone so far as to declare which languages are considered to be classical languages. These are the languages you'd find used in ancient Indian texts and literature. People who are interested in reading these tests would need to learn one of these classical languages and not some later form of it. The following languages have received "classical" status by the Indian government: Malayalam, Telugu, Kannada, Tamil, Odia, and Sanskrit.

Overall, India has become a popular tourist destination amongst westerners because of how much the English language has been integrated into Indian society. If you go to a major Indian cities like Kolkata or New Delhi, then you will likely be able to speak to all the Indian people you come across in your native English language. This makes it extremely convenient and more comfortable for westerners which, in turn, help boost the Indian economy at the same time. The irony here is that the British rule over India actually helped it later on because it integrated the English language into the Indian culture and that helped it thrive economically.

Hindi for fun – Learn some basic Hindi

Hello – Namaste

How are you – Aap kaise hai

What is your name – Aap ka kya naam hai

My name is John – Mera naam John hai

Where are you from – Aap kaha se aaye hai

Pleased to meet you – Aap se mill ke bahut khusi hui

I am going – Mai jaa raha hu (male), Mai jaa rahi hu (female)

Where are you from – Aap kaha se hai

Do you speak English – Kyaa aap English bolte hai

Thank you – Dhanyevaad

Sorry – Maaf kijiye

Where is the hotel – Hotel kaha hai

Stop – Ruko

Hot – Garam

Cold - Thanda

What is the time – Samay kya hua hai

Water – Paani

Food – Khana

Friend – Dost

Hello friend – Namaste dost

Please – Kripya

I am fine – Mai thik hu

Yes – Haan

No – Nahi

Help – Madad

See you later – Phir milenge

How much is this – Ye kitnay ka hai

I need to go – Mujhe jaana hai

One minute – Ek minute

Okay – Thik hai

I don't know – Mujhe nahi maloom

Chapattis – Roti

Vegetables – Subji

Potato Aaloo

Tea- Chai

Can I have tea – Mujhe chai chahiye

Popular Festivals of India

All the diversity in India brings a variety of interesting festivals and activities to the cities and towns of the country. The Indian people take their festivals seriously and put a lot of passion and emotion into the preparation and celebration of them. These festivals are so memorable that even foreigners from other countries come to India just to watch them. In India, the festivals are typically divided into three categories. There are seasonal festivals, religious festivals, and national festivals. Each individual festival has its own special meaning and significance behind it. Although the foreigners who watch the festivals might not understand the meaning, it can certainly be seen in the eyes of the locals who are celebrating them.

The three main national festivals of India are Independence Day, Republic Day and Gandhi Jayanti. The nation's Independence Day is obviously not celebrated on the same day that it is in the United States because the holiday has a different history behind it for each country. India's Independence Day is celebrated on August 15th of each year and it signifies the day in 1947 when Indians took its country back from the British Empire and finally became its own independent nation. Some people even refer to it as India Day because of this meaning. Republic Day is celebrated on January 26th of each year and it signifies the day in 1950 when India introduced its constitution of laws which govern the country. Festivals on this day will play "Jana Gana Mana,' which is the country's national song. Gandhi Jayanti is a national holiday that takes place on October 2nd, which is the day that Mahatma Gandhi was born. He is considered to be the "Father of the Nation" because of his efforts to bring freedom and independence to India. The song "Raghupati Raghav" is played on this day, which was Gandhi's favorite song when he was alive.

There are numerous religion festivals that take place all year in the country. Some of the most popular ones include Diwali, Holi, Christmas, Ram Navami, Krishna Janmaashtami, Mahavir Jayanti, Eid, Buddha Purnima and Maha Shivaratri. Diwali, for example, is a Hindu festival that is celebrated to honor how good has defeated evil and how brightness is stronger than darkness. Hindus are honoring Lord Ram's return to the Ayodhya kingdom after he bravely defeated the Demon King "Ravana" and saved his wife Sita from him. Some people refer to this holiday as the "Festival of Lights" because there are so many fireworks that go off and clay lamps that are lit as part of the celebration.

India also likes to celebrate the changing of the seasons, especially when it is the time that crops can be harvested. The seasonal festivals they conduct include Baisakhi, Onam, Lohri, Basant Panchami, Makar Sankranti, and Pongal. The most popular seasonal festival is Onam and it is celebrated for ten days. It is supposed to symbolize the return of King Mahabali, who is an ancient king of Hindu mythology. The people who celebrate this festival will place beautiful flower arrangements on the ground around their home as a way to welcome the king back to his homeland. People will often wear new clothes and have magnificent feasts that are served on banana leaves. There will also be snake boat races, games, sports and dancing activities being conducted as well.

You can find festivals being celebrated all throughout the year in India. The national festivals are more symbolic to the history of the nation while the other festivals have a spiritual essence to them. Either way, you will enjoy watching these festivals no matter who you are because they are filled with passion and excitement that you won't find anywhere else.

Ramayana – Epic story of right and wrong

Epic poetry was a popular form of literature to come out of ancient India. Ramayana is one of the most recognized epic poems to come out of ancient India. It was written in Sanskrit, which is an ancient Indic language that originated in India and was used to write numerous classical epic poems and Hindu scriptures. As for Ramayana, it is a poem that helped influence the Indian civilization throughout the centuries. The only other epic poem that is just as important to the Indian people is Mahabharata. These two epic poems hold the same importance to Hindus as the Koran does to the Muslims or the Holy Bible does to Christians. The Ramayana and the Mahabharata are often read together in a collection known as Itihasa.

Historians are not sure exactly when the Ramayana was first created, but evidence shows that it might have existed in oral form around the year 1,500 B.C. In those days, most stories and poems were only told through voice rather than through written words. It wasn't until the 4th century B.C. that a poet named Valmiki actually wrote out the Ramayana in Sanskrit. The Ramayana tells the story of a prince named Rama who struggles to rescue his wife, Sita, from the clutches of the demon king named Ravana. It is written as a narrative of Rama's life from the perspective of the author.

According to legend, Rama was a prince of the Kosala Kingdom and then later believed to be an avatar of Lord Vishnu. Rama's father was King Dasharatha and he ended up banishing his son from the Kosala Kingdom. Rama, his brother Lakshmana, and Sita were all traveling together throughout the forests of India while trying to find their way. That was when they came across the evil Ravana who ended up kidnapping Sita. Rama declared war against Ravana and then ultimately defeated him in the end, getting his wife back in the process. Rama went back to Ayodhya, which was the capital of Kosala Kingdom, and became the new king of the kingdom. This victory of good over evil has been celebrated by Hindus for thousands of years. The five-day Diwali festival is conducted each year to celebrate Rama's victory over the demon king. People who have read the Ramayana will truly understand its significance and why Hindus are so passionate about celebrating it.

Out of all the world's literature, the Ramayana is considered to be one of the biggest epics of ancient history. As a poem, it has almost 24,000 verses to it which are split into 7 different books (or Kandas) and has as many as 500 chapters. Hindus consider the Ramayana to be the first poem, or the adi-kavya. The poem teaches Hindus about the duties of relationships and how these relationships shape the lives of these characters The Ramayana portrays the royal family as ideal characters. There is the ideal prince, the ideal king, the ideal servant, the ideal father, the ideal wife and the ideal brother. This poem has not only influenced the lives and culture of Hindus, but it has influenced other Sanskrit literature as well. Everything from its ethical elements to its philosophical elements is taught to Hindus who study it. Then they take those elements and apply them to their life in the modern age.

Like many ancient forms of literature, the Ramayana has multiple versions throughout the world. These versions tend to have some major differences between each other, which ends making cultures that look upon this book a little bit different than each other. North India and South India is one example of this because the Ramayana that exists in these regions are a bit different than each other. The poem is also still told orally in Thailand, Philippines, Cambodia, Indonesia, Maldives, Vietnam, Laos, and Malaysia. In total, there is said to be 300 different versions of Ramayana around the world.

Mahabharata - The ancient epic poem of India

The Mahabharata is the name of the second major epic poem of ancient India that was written in Sanskrit, the first poem being the famous "Ramayana." The Mahabharata was an important influence on Hinduism and its development between the years 400 B.C. and 200 A.D. This epic poem is about the Hindu moral law known as "Dharma" and the history of the Kurukshetra War.

The Mahabharata also tells the story of how two sets of cousins were struggling for sovereignty in their kingdom. One group of cousins was the Pandavas, who were the sons of King Pandu, and the other group of cousins was the Kauravas, who were the sons of King Dhritarashtra. Most importantly, the Mahabharata teaches about the four goals of life that we should all strive for. These goals are represented by the word "purusartha," and are for dharma, Artha, Kama, and Moksa. Dharma is the symbol of morality and righteousness, Artha is the symbol of economic value and prosperity, Kama is the symbol of love and pleasure, and Moksa is the symbol of spiritual value and liberation. These are the four goals that all Hindus try to achieve even to this day.

Each of the four goals is important, but they are not always
achievable. In times of crisis or conflict, a Hindu will focus on
Dharma above all else. This means that a Hindu would be
willing to sacrifice their love and wealth if it meant doing what
was morally right. This, in turn, will bring them their spiritual
liberation even in death. Of course, this isn't always easy for
some Hindus because the temptations of love and wealth can
be quite powerful. This forces some Hindus to renounce all
forms of pleasure and wealth just so they can at least have
Dharma, since that is more important to them.

Vyasa is believed to be the author of the Mahabharata. He also happens to be a character in the poem as well. This makes him a truly central figure in the Hindu religion. He is also believed to be the one who scribed the Puranas and Vedas texts that were written in Sanskrit. As for the Mahabharata, the oldest preserved written text of this story is thought to be from around the year 400 B.C. However, historians theorize that the story was actually created around the 8th or 9th century B.C. During this period, it was a story that was likely spoken to people orally and had no written form whatsoever. It wasn't until the Gupta period of the 4th century A.D. that the complete version of the Mahabharata was made available in written format.

The Mahabharata has a reputation for being the longest poem ever written. It contains more than 200,000 lines of verses, or 100,000 shloka lines (each shloka has two verses). A word count on the poem shows that it has roughly 1.8 million words in total. This makes the Mahabharata ten times longer than the two famous Greek epic poems called the Odyssey and the Iliad. It is even four times longer than Ramayana, which is the first epic poem of Hinduism. The importance of the Mahabharata to the Hindus can be compared to the importance of William Shakespeare's books, the Holy Bible, the Qur'an and the literature of Homer.

The Mahabharata poem has been rewritten and retold countless times over the last two thousand years. This has sparked multiple versions of the story to exist in various regions throughout southern Asia. Some of the writings are sculpted into stone, like Cambodia's Angkor Thom and Angkor Wat. Some miniature Indian paintings will have some of the poem's content as well.

The Taj Mahal

The one Indian landmark that everyone has heard of is the Taj Mahal. It is a mausoleum made of ivory-white marble and it is located on the southern bank of the Yamuna River, which is located in the city of Agra. The order to have the Taj Mahal built was originally given by Mughal emperor Shah Jahan in 1632. Jahan wanted the mausoleum built so that he could house his dead wife's remains there. Jahan cherished his wife and he was absolutely crushed when she died. Although he had multiple wives in his lifetime, he considered his wife Mumtaz Mahal to be his favorite wife.

The Taj Mahal is about 42 acres in size. The tomb of Mumtaz Mahal is the centerpiece of the mausoleum and it also contains a guest house and mosque. The outside has a series of formal gardens with a crenelated wall surrounding it on three sides. When the construction of it was commissioned in 1632, it took about eleven years for the main architecture of it to be completed. It still took another ten years after that for the Taj Mahal to be completely finished. It is estimated that it cost about 32 million rupees to construct the entire complex. This would be equal to about 53 billion rupees in today's currency, or $827 million USD. Emperor Jahan had as many as 20,000 artisans working on the construction. They were all under the direction of Ustad Ahmad Lahauri, who was emperor's court architect and leader of the board of architects who oversaw the Taj Mahal's construction.

Nowadays the Taj Mahal is a tourist attraction that brings millions of people to visit it each year. In 1983, the United Nations declared the Taj Mahal to be a World Heritage Site. It is the most impressive Mughal architecture to ever exist and has become symbolic of the rich history that India has had. Even if you aren't familiar with the name Taj Mahal, you've probably at least seen a picture of it before somewhere. The top of it contains a marble dome with a bunch of smaller domes around it. There are even decorative spires on the base walls which extend from the edges. Around the Taj Mahal building, there are four minarets which help form the central building and the tomb that is in it.

There is certainly no other piece of architecture in the world quite like the Taj Mahal. Everyone should view it at least one time in their life because it is the most beautiful structure in the world.

Traditional dresses of India

What is fascinating about India is that its richly diverse
cultures and traditions bring variety to just about all aspects of
Indian life. You will see diversity in food, languages, and
clothing as you travel to different regions of India. Traditional
dresses, for example, come in all different looks and styles,
and you may not be able to tell that they're traditional if
you're not educated on classic Indian attire. Let's look at some
of the most popular traditional Indian dresses.

When westerners hear the word "dress," they typically think
of a dress for a woman that wraps around the legs. But
dresses in India are so diverse that there are some available
for men as well as women. The Kurta-Pyjama is one example

of a dress that is worn by a man. In fact, these dresses are worn by men all throughout India. It basically consists of a long shirt that hangs down far below the waist. If the person is wearing a pathani suit, then they'll usually be wearing baggy white pants along with it. You'll see these outfits being worn a lot in festivals and other special celebratory occasions.

A dress that is worn by both sexes in India is the lungi. It is a loincloth made of cotton or silk and can be worn all year round, even during the dreadfully hot summer days. You'll also see men wearing them in bhangra dances and during festivals and ceremonies. They are the traditional form of attire in South India.

If you ever go to a village in India, you will usually find the villagers wearing dhotis. A dhoti is a dress traditionally worn by Hindu men and boys. It is a garment that ties around the person's waist and it stretches all the way down to the person's feet. Hindus used to just wear the dhoti with nothing else to cover their upper body. But nowadays, Hindu men can be seen wearing a sherwani in combination with the dhoti when they attend special ceremonies such as weddings.

The Pheran is a full-length gown that originated in the region of India known as Kashmir. Men and women both wear this dress, but you'll typically see men wearing it more in the wintertime. A dress that is more popular with women is the Puanchei. This dress originated in the northeastern Indian state called Mizoram. Women wear this dress to festivals and wedding ceremonies mostly. If they are performing the popular Bamboo dance, they'll wear the Puanchei along with a blouse called the kawrechi.

Heavier attire such as coats has originated in northern India because of the colder climate. The Sherwani is a coat that men wear when they are going to a formal get together or occasion. If it is really cold out, then a man may wear the knee length version of this coat which is called the Achkan. Mostly, you'll see men in northern India wearing these but they are also becoming popular in the south as well.

The sari is one of the most popular dresses amongst women in South Asia. Over the years, the sari has undergone various alterations based on the evolution of various cultures. This has sparked multiple versions of the sari such as the silk sari, kanjivaram sari, banarasi sari, patola sari, and so on. The one similar feature of these saris is that it drapes down at various places. However, where it drapes down is what makes them different. Saris have a loose end called a pallu. With some saris, they drape down with the pallu on the back while others have it with the pallu on the front. Either way, it makes an Indian woman look elegant.

Message from the author

Thank you for reading my book. I request you to share that you've read my book on your Facebook, Twitter and/or LinkedIn accounts to spread the word about this book so that more people will be able to take advantage of the information presented in this book.

I hope I've been helpful. If you need further advice or information, you can contact me from my website http://www.shalusharma.com or you can tweet me at https://twitter.com/bihar. You can always connect with me on Twitter or email info@ShaluSharma.com. Don't hesitate to get in touch any time or ask a question. I will try my best to answer any questions that you might have. You can find my other books here http://www.amazon.com/author/shalusharma

60653814R10043

Made in the USA
Columbia, SC
16 June 2019